Gloucestersh...

Items should b...
on or before...

OLIVER TWIST

RETOLD BY PAULINE FRANCIS

Published by Evans Brothers Limited
2A Portman Mansions
Chiltern Street
London W1U 6NR

British Library Cataloguing in Publication data
Francis, Pauline
  Oliver Twist. – (Fast track classics)
    1.Orphans – England – London – Juvenile fiction 2.London
    (England) – Social life and customs – 19th century –
    Juvenile fiction 3.Children's stories
    I. Title II.Dickens, Charles, 1812-1870. Oliver Twist
    823.9'14[J]
    ISBN 0237525372

OLIVER TWIST

Introduction

Charles Dickens was born in 1812, the second of eight children. When he was twelve years old, his father went to prison because he owed money. Charles went out to work to help his family. He never forgot this terrible time when he was poor, and later used his experiences in some of his stories.

In his twenties, Charles found work writing about London life for newspapers and magazines. Some of these articles were published as a book called *Pickwick Papers*. This is how Charles Dickens became famous at the age of twenty-four.

A year later, Charles began to write the story of Oliver Twist as a monthly magazine serial. It was published as a book in 1838. *Oliver Twist* tells the story of a poor orphan, Oliver, who survives starvation and life with the evil Fagin. Fagin, by training Oliver to be a pickpocket, does his best to destroy the young boy's childish innocence.

Charles Dickens wrote many more famous novels, including *Nicholas Nickleby*, *David Copperfield*, *A Christmas Carol* and *Great Expectations*. He died in 1870 at the age of fifty-eight and is buried in Westminster Abbey, London.

CHAPTER ONE

Hungry!

In the workhouse of a small town north of London, a pale young woman raised her head feebly from her pillow. She touched a locket around her neck, then the ring on her finger. "Give these to the child," she said to the nurse by her bed.

"I will, my dear," the old woman replied.

The nurse placed the newborn baby into its mother's arms. The young woman kissed its forehead with her cold white lips, shuddered – and died.

"Where did she come from?" the doctor asked.

"Nobody knows," the nurse said.

Oliver cried loudly. And if he had known that he was an orphan, he would probably have cried even louder...

After his birth, Oliver was sent to an orphanage where he had to live on the smallest amount of food possible. There he grew into a pale, thin child. On his ninth birthday, Mr Bumble, who looked after the orphans for the parish church, came to see him.

"Oliver is too old to stay here," he told the old woman who ran the orphanage. "It's time he went to live in the workhouse where he will be taught a useful trade. Then he can earn his keep. Let me see him at once."

Mr Bumble had to wait a long time. He did not know that Oliver was spending his birthday in the coal-cellar. Why? He had dared to complain that he was hungry!

"Will you come with me, Oliver?" Mr Bumble asked gently when the boy came into the room.

Oliver, hearing the kindness in the man's voice, took his chance. He began to cry. "I am hungry," he wept.

"Bring him some bread!" Mr Bumble ordered.

With two slices of bread and butter in his hand and a small brown parish cap on his head, Oliver went with Mr Bumble. He was glad to leave that wretched house where no kind word or look had ever brightened the gloom of his early years.

There was one rule in the workhouse – all the poor people who lived there had to starve slowly! They were given oatmeal and water three times a day, an onion twice a week and half a bread roll on Sundays.

"Somebody will have to ask for more," one of the boys said. "We shall draw lots." It was Oliver who picked the short straw. That evening, when all the boys had emptied their bowls, they winked at Oliver. He got up from the table and held his empty bowl out to the master.

"Please, sir, I want some more," he said.

There was a long silence.

"What!" the astonished man said at last.

"Please, sir, I want some more," Oliver said again.

The master picked up a big spoon and beat Oliver about the head. "Mr Bumble!" he shouted. "Oliver Twist has asked for more!"

Oliver was locked up alone in a room. When night came, he put his hands over his eyes to shut out the darkness. The next morning, this notice appeared on the gate of the workhouse.

REWARD
£5 to take boy in as an apprentice

At last, a week later, Mr Bumble unlocked the door of the room. "You are going to work for Mr Sowerberry, the undertaker," he told Oliver. "Now put your cap on straight and hold up your head, boy."

"Yes, sir," Oliver replied in a trembling voice.

They reached Mr Sowerberry's shop just as he was closing up the shutters on the windows. The shopkeeper lifted up his candle to look at Oliver. "Mrs Sowerberry!" he called. "He's here!"

Mrs Sowerberry came from a little room behind the shop and peered closely at Oliver. "Dear me!" she said, "he is very small."

"He'll grow, Mrs Sowerberry," Mr Bumble replied.

"I dare say he will," she grumbled, "and eat and drink us out of the house." She opened a small door. "Get down there, little bag o' bones!" she cried.

She pushed Oliver down a steep flight of stairs into a dark kitchen where an untidy girl sat by the fire. "Charlotte," Mrs Sowerberry shouted as she followed him. "Give this boy some of the cold bits o' meat the dog didn't want."

Oliver's eyes lit up at the thought of some meat. It was awful to see how eagerly he tore that terrible food apart. When he had finished it, Mrs Sowerberry picked up a dim lamp and led the way back upstairs. "You won't mind sleeping among the coffins, I suppose?" she asked. "It doesn't matter whether you do or don't. Your bed's under the counter."

Oliver worked very hard at the undertakers and his sad face was just right for attending funerals. At the end of a month's trial, Mr Sowerberry took him on as an apprentice undertaker. He would have been almost happy if it hadn't have been for Noah.

Noah Claypole also worked for Mr Sowerberry. He was jealous of Oliver and treated him badly. One day, when Oliver and Noah went down to the kitchen to eat, Noah began to tease Oliver. He pulled his hair and tweaked his ears.

"Sneak!" he hissed. "I'd like to see yer hanged!"

Oliver did not let himself cry.

"How's yer mother?" Noah asked at last.

"She's dead," Oliver replied, his cheeks turning red. "Don't say anything about her to me!"

"Yer mother was a real bad 'un," Noah sneered.

"What did you say?" Oliver asked angrily.

"A bad 'un," Noah repeated, "and it were a good thing she died before she was hung."

Red with anger, Oliver jumped up and seized Noah by the throat. He shook him until his teeth chattered in his head. Then, with one great blow, he knocked him to the floor.

"Charlotte!" Noah cried. "The new boy's murdering me! Help! Help! Oliver's gone mad! Charlotte!"

Charlotte and Mrs Sowerberry rushed in and dragged Oliver, struggling and shouting, away from the other boy. Then Mr Sowerberry beat him with a stick. That night, when he was finally left alone, Oliver wept before falling into a troubled sleep. He awoke as the first ray of light glinted through the gaps in the shutters across the shop window.

"I am not going to let them beat me any more," he thought proudly. "I shall run away and seek my fortune a long way from here."

Oliver got up and unlocked the door. Then, looking quickly from right to left, he went outside and set off up the hill.

CHAPTER TWO
Fagin takes Oliver in

As soon as Oliver reached the road, he began to run, hiding in the hedgerows every time somebody passed by. At last, he came to a milestone: LONDON 70 miles.

"I shall go there!" he thought. "It's so big that nobody will find me!"

Oliver went twenty miles that day. He ate only a dry crust of bread and some water. When night came, he turned into a field and crept under a bundle of hay. He felt frightened at first, but he was so tired that he soon fell asleep.

The next day, he could walk only twelve miles because his feet were sore and his legs were so weak that they trembled. Some people were very kind and gave him scraps of bread and cheese. He stumbled on for several days until, at last, he arrived in the little town of Barnet, a few miles north of London. It was so early that all the shops were still closed. Oliver sat on a cold doorstep to rest. A boy, wearing a man's coat nearly down to the ground, came over to him. He was short, with bowed legs, and sharp, ugly eyes.

"What's the matter?" the boy asked.

"I am very hungry and tired," Oliver told him with

tears in his eyes. "I have been walking for seven days."

"You want grub, you shall have it," the boy replied, dragging Oliver to his feet." My name's Jack Dawkins – but my friends call me the Artful Dodger because I'm good at avoiding trouble. Call me Dodger for short."

The Dodger took Oliver to an inn.

"Going to London?" the Dodger asked as they tucked into ham, bread and beer.

"Yes," Oliver said.

"Got any lodgings? Any money?" he asked.

Oliver shook his head.

"I suppose you want a place to sleep tonight?" the Dodger said.

"I do," Oliver replied.

"I've got to be in London tonight and I know a respectable old gentleman wot'll give you lodgings for nothink," the Dodger told him.

The Dodger didn't want to reach London before dark, so it was nearly eleven o'clock when they came to the outskirts of the city. Oliver glanced around him. He had never seen a more wretched place. The street was very narrow and muddy and filled with terrible smells. There were dirty, screaming children crawling everywhere. The side streets were full of drunken men and women. Just as Oliver was wondering whether to run away again, his friend opened the door of a house and pulled him inside.

"What's the password?" a voice called out.

"Plummy and slam!" the Dodger replied.

The Dodger pulled Oliver firmly up the stairs behind him, and into a room at the back of the house. This room was black with age and dirt and lit by a candle stuck in a ginger-beer bottle. A very old and shrivelled man stood at the fire, cooking sausages. His ugly face was half-covered by his matted red hair.

Oliver glanced at a clothes-horse at the man's side. It was hanging with silk handkerchiefs. Several rough beds, made of old sacks, were huddled side by side on the floor. Seated around the table were four or five boys, smoking long clay pipes and drinking gin in hot water.

"Fagin, this is my friend Oliver Twist," the Dodger said.

"Pleased to make your acquaintance, Mr Twist," Fagin said, bowing. "I see you're staring at the handkerchiefs. We've just got them out to wash, Oliver, that's all."

To Oliver's surprise, Fagin and the boys began to laugh loudly. He sat down with them and ate a large supper, drank some gin with hot water and fell into a deep sleep. When he woke up the next morning, he was alone in the room with Fagin. Half-asleep, he lay watching the old man as he placed a small box on the table. Fagin's eyes shone as he lifted the lid and took out a gold watch, brooches, bracelets and other jewellery.

"Why does he live in such a dirty place if he is so rich?" Oliver asked himself.

When the other boys came in, bringing more silk handkerchiefs, Fagin played a very strange game with them. He put a watch in his waistcoat pocket and trotted up and down the room, stopping from time to time as if he were looking in a shop window. The Dodger and a boy called Charley followed him closely. Suddenly, the Dodger trod on Fagin's toes and Charley fell against him. A second later, the boys held up Fagin's watch!

In the afternoon, two young ladies came to visit. They were not very pretty, but their faces were bright with powder and lipstick. One of them was called Nancy and

Oliver liked her very much. After drinking some gin, they went out with the Dodger and Charley.

"Do what those boys tell you and you'll do well in life, Oliver," Fagin muttered as he came over to Oliver. "Now, is my handkerchief hanging out of my pocket, my dear?"

"Yes, sir," Oliver replied.

"See if you can take it out without my knowing, like the boys did this morning," Fagin said.

Oliver held up the bottom of the pocket with one hand, as he had seen the Dodger hold it, and pulled the handkerchief gently out with the other.

"You're a clever boy, my dear," Fagin said, patting

Oliver's head. "Here's a shilling for you. You'll be a great man one day."

"What has taking a handkerchief out of an old man's pocket to do with being a great man?" Oliver thought.

Oliver stayed in that room for many days. Sometimes he took part in the games he had watched that first morning. But he soon grew bored.

"May I go outside, sir?" he asked Fagin one day. "I want some fresh air and I have nothing to do."

"Yes, my dear," Fagin replied, smiling to himself. "You may go out with Dodger and Charley today."

When the boys had been walking in the street for some time, the Dodger began to act strangely. He pulled Oliver and Charley close to him, put his finger to his lips and pointed to an old man at a bookstall. Then the Dodger and Charley crept up behind the man. Oliver, mystified, followed them. To his horror, he saw the Dodger plunge his hand into the gentleman's pocket and pull out a silk handkerchief. Then he and Charley ran away at top speed.

"Now I know why Fagin had all those watches and handkerchiefs and jewels!" Oliver gasped.

Oliver froze on the spot, staring in horror. Close by, a tall man wrapped in a long cloak caught sight of him. And he, too, gasped with horror.

CHAPTER THREE
Kidnapped

At last, Oliver began to run. At the same moment, the old gentleman put his hand to his pocket, missed his handkerchief and saw Oliver.

"Stop thief!" he shouted.

Everybody joined in the chase, even the Dodger and Charley. Somebody hit Oliver and he fell into the dust. Then a policeman seized him by the collar.

"It wasn't me, sir," Oliver cried, "it was those two."

But the Dodger and Charley had already run off. The policeman dragged Oliver to the police station, followed by the old gentleman.

"My name is Mr Brownlow," the old gentleman told the officer at the desk. "I'm not sure now whether this boy did take my handkerchief. I do not want you to charge him. He looks ill, poor child."

He stared hard at Oliver. "There is something about that boy's face…" he thought to himself. "He looks like… no, I cannot remember who it is."

Poor Oliver, dizzy with fear, was pulled towards one of the prison cells. Suddenly, a man ran into the office.

"Stop!" he cried. "Don't take him away! I own the bookstall. Those other boys committed the robbery."

"The boy is free to go!" the police officer shouted. "Clear the office."

When Mr Brownlow went outside, he found little Oliver Twist already lying on the pavement, his face deadly white. He called a carriage which took them to a neat house in a quiet street in north London. There, Oliver slept for many days. At last, he was well enough to go downstairs. As he sat eating by the fire, he stared at a painting hanging on the wall opposite his chair.

"What a beautiful face!" he said. "Who is that lady?"

"Nobody that you or I know," the housekeeper, Mrs Bedwin, replied.

"She is very pretty," Oliver said. "Her eyes seem to stare as if she were alive and wanted to speak to me."

"Don't say such strange things, child!" Mrs Bedwin cried. "You're still weak and nervous after your illness. I'll turn your chair round so that you can't see it."

Mr Brownlow came into the room. "I am happy to see you looking so much better, young man," he said.

He stared at Oliver for a moment, then at the painting behind the boy.

"Good gracious!" he said. "They have the same eyes, nose and mouth. Even their expression is the same!"

Oliver's heart started to beat faster, although he did not know why, and he fainted.

The next day, the painting was no longer there. "Why

have they taken it away?" Oliver cried. "I liked it."

"Mr Brownlow thought it might worry you," Mrs Bedwin told him, "and stop you from getting well again."

They were happy days for Oliver because everybody was so kind and gentle. About a week after his arrival, Mr Brownlow sent for Oliver.

"Don't send me away, sir!" Oliver begged. "Let me stay here and be your servant. Please, sir."

"My dear child," Mr Brownlow said, moved by Oliver's words. "I shall not do that. I feel that I can trust you. Now tell me about yourself."

Oliver began his story. He had just reached the part where Mr Bumble took him off to the workhouse when a man from the bookstall delivered some new books.

"Quickly, go after him, Mrs Bedwin!" Mr Brownlow called as he heard her close the door again. "You have forgotten that I need to pay him!"

"Oh, let me go for you, sir," Oliver said.

Oliver was running along the street, thinking how happy he was, when a young girl came up to him and threw her arms around his neck. "I've found him, Bill!" she shouted to a man standing in a doorway. "You naughty boy, Oliver! Come home now."

As he struggled to get away, Oliver saw the girl's face for the first time. "Nancy!" he cried in surprise. "What are you doing here? Let me go!"

Bill, followed by his dog Bull's-eye, came over to Oliver and struck his head violently. Terrified by the growling of the dog and weak from his illness, Oliver stopped struggling. He let himself be dragged by Nancy and Bill along the streets until they reached a house.

"Here he is, Mr Fagin!" a boy inside cried.

When Oliver found himself back in that dirty dark room, he ran out through the door crying for help. Fagin and the Dodger went after him. Bill Sikes began to untie Bull's-eye but Nancy caught hold of his arm.

"Hold the dog back, Bill," she shouted. "He'll tear the boy to pieces."

"Serves him right!" Sikes replied. "Now let go of me!"

"I shan't let that child be torn to pieces by a dog!" Nancy shrieked, struggling with him. Sikes threw Nancy to the floor just as Fagin and the Dodger came back with Oliver.

"So you wanted to get away, did you, my dear?" Fagin said, picking up a wooden club from the fireplace. "We'll soon cure you of that, my boy."

He hit Oliver hard. Nancy ran forward, snatched the club from his hand and threw it into the fire with such force that some of the hot coals fell into the room.

"I wish I'd been shot dead before I was forced to bring him back here," Nancy shouted.

Then she fell to the floor, sobbing.

CHAPTER FOUR
An evil plan

A few days later, Mr Bumble arrived in London on business. No sooner had he eaten breakfast at his inn when this newspaper advertisement caught his eye:

FIVE GUINEAS REWARD FOR THE RETURN OF OLIVER TWIST

This reward will be paid to anyone who can give information leading to his safe return or to anyone who can give information about this boy's life. The boy is small and thin and wears a brown cap.

Mr Brownlow

Mr Bumble made his way straight to the address given. Mr Brownlow welcomed him warmly. "Do you know where this poor boy is now?" he asked.

Mr Bumble shook his head.

"Well, what do you know?" Mr Brownlow cried.

"He is an orphan brought up in the workhouse," Mr Bumble said. "He has always been an ungrateful boy."

"I thought I could trust him," said Mr Brownlow sadly.

When Mr Bumble had gone, clutching his reward, Mr Brownlow told Mrs Bedwin what he had learned.

"I will never believe it, sir," she said. "He was a dear, gentle and grateful child."

"Silence!" Mr Brownlow cried. "Never let me hear that boy's name again!"

Mr Bumble was not the only one to call Oliver ungrateful that day. As soon as the other boys had gone out to work, Fagin caught him by the arm.

"I took you in when you was hungry," he muttered angrily. "I had another young lad who was ungrateful like you and he went to talk to the police. He was hanged, Oliver. I hope you never has to hang, my dear boy."

Oliver's blood ran cold as he listened. His arms and legs trembled. Fagin patted Oliver's head. "If you keep quiet and work hard, we shall be good friends," he said.

Fagin picked up his hat and coat and went out, locking the door behind him. Oliver saw no one from morning until midnight. In this way, Fagin made Oliver prefer the company of thieves to his own sad thoughts.

One chilly, damp evening, Fagin buttoned up his overcoat and stepped outside into the muddy street. A black mist hung everywhere. Fagin walked until he came to a maze of narrow streets and entered a house there.

"Who is it?" a voice called out.

"Only me, Bill, only me," Fagin replied.

Fagin went inside. Nancy was there too, warming her feet by the fire. Fagin sat down close to Bill Sikes.

"What about that house, Bill?" he whispered. "When are we going to steal all that lovely silver?"

"We're not," Sikes said sharply. "None of the servants there will help us. Will yer pay me fifty extra pounds to break in?" he asked. "I shall need a small boy."

Fagin nodded and glanced at Nancy.

"Fetch me a jug of beer, Nancy," Sikes said.

"You don't need any beer," she replied. "I know what's in Fagin's mind. Go on, tell Bill about Oliver."

"Ha! You're a clever one, my dear," Fagin said. "It's true – I was going to speak about the boy. It's time he began to earn his keep. He'll do anything for you, Bill, if you frighten him."

"If he doesn't do what I tell him, you won't see him alive again," Sikes replied. He pulled out a crowbar and waved it about. "Bring him tomorrow night," he cried.

CHAPTER FIVE
The robbery

When Oliver woke up in the morning, he was surprised to see a new pair of shoes by the side of his bed.

"Are you letting me go?" he asked Fagin.

"Yes," the old man replied. "You are going to Bill Sikes' house tonight."

"Why?" Oliver asked.

"Wait till he tells you," Fagin said.

Nancy came for Oliver at eleven o'clock that night. She was very pale and Oliver realised that he had some power over her feelings. Perhaps she would let him escape! But the girl guessed his thoughts. She pointed to the bruises on her neck and arms. "I have promised Bill that you will come with me quietly," she told him. "If you do not, you will come to harm, and so will I."

A carriage was waiting outside which took them quickly through the dark streets to Sikes' house. When they reached his room, Sikes pulled off Oliver's cap and sat him at the table. Then he picked up his pistol and put it to Oliver's forehead.

"If yer speak one word when we're out tomorrow, except when I speak to you, I'll blow yer brains out," Sikes said. "Now let's have a snooze before we go."

Oliver lay awake for a long time watching Nancy sitting by the fire. Then, weary from worry, he fell asleep. It was almost morning when the rain beating against the window woke him up. Bill Sikes hurried him from the house. They walked all day until they reached an old house out in the countryside. Sikes pushed Oliver through the door and they entered a low dark room.

"This is the boy," Sikes said to his friend, Toby Crackit.

Crackit grinned and poured gin and water into three glasses. "Here's to our success!" he said. "Drink up, boy."

Frightened, Oliver drank too quickly and fell into a deep sleep. At half past one in the morning, Crackit woke him up. He and Sikes wrapped their heads and shoulders in large dark shawls, put on their overcoats, picked up their pistols and dragged Oliver out of the house.

It was now very dark and the fog was much thicker. They walked for about half an hour until they stopped in front of a large house surrounded by a wall. Crackit climbed quickly to the top, then pulled Oliver up behind him. The poor boy was almost mad with terror as he realised what was happening. "Robbery and murder!" he gasped in horror. "That's why I am here!"

His trembling legs would not hold him as he was dragged towards the house. He fell to the ground.

"Get up!" Sikes whispered, shaking with rage. "Get up or I'll blow yer brains over the grass!"

"Oh, please let me go!" Oliver cried. "Let me run away and die in a field! Please do not make me steal."

Sikes pressed his pistol against Oliver's head, but Crackit knocked it away.

"Hush!" he said. "But if you say another word, boy, I'll kill you myself. Now force that shutter open, Bill."

Sikes picked up his crowbar and opened the shutter of a small window at the back of the house. It was just large enough for a small boy like Oliver.

"Now, listen," Sikes whispered, pulling a lantern from his pocket. "I'm going to lift you through the window. Take this lantern and go quietly up the stairs into the hall. Go to the door and open it for us."

Sikes pushed Oliver through the window. "If you stop, I'll shoot you!" he whispered. "Now, go!"

Oliver made his way slowly towards the stairs.

"Come back!" Sikes cried suddenly.

Scared by the sudden noise of Sikes' voice, Oliver dropped his lantern and froze on the spot. A light appeared at the top of the stairs and two terrified men appeared in the doorway. There was a loud bang and a flash of light. Oliver staggered back. Before the smoke had cleared away, Sikes leaned through the window and dragged Oliver towards him. Oliver heard the noise of a pistol again and men shouting. Then a cold feeling crept over him, and he saw and heard no more.

CHAPTER SIX
Faces at the window

Towards dawn, the rain came down, thick and fast, pattering on the leafless bushes. But Oliver did not hear it. He lay helpless and unconscious at the bottom of a ditch where Sikes had thrown him as he ran away.

At last, a cry of pain woke him up. Oliver looked at his left arm. It hung heavy and useless at his side, wrapped roughly in a blood-soaked shawl. He was so weak that he could hardly sit up.

"They've left me here to die," he thought. "I must get help."

Oliver got up and managed to stagger to the road. The rain began to fall more heavily and it stopped him from fainting again. He dragged himself towards a house surrounded by a high wall. As he came closer, he remembered that he had been there during the night. He was so afraid that he tried to run away. But he could hardly stand. Instead, he swayed across the lawn, knocked faintly at the door and slithered to the ground.

At this very moment, the servants were in the kitchen talking about the attempted robbery. As they opened the door slowly and carefully, all they saw was poor little Oliver Twist, speechless and exhausted, looking at them with begging eyes. One of the servants caught hold of him.

"Here's the thief, Miss Rose!" he shouted up the stairs. "I shot him, miss."

"Hush," Miss Rose called back. "You'll frighten my aunt as much as the thieves did. Now take the poor boy up to your room and send for the doctor."

Oliver slept until the evening. As he lay there, Miss Rose and her aunt, Mrs Maylie, came to see him. They expected to see a wild ruffian. Instead, they saw a young child, worn out with pain.

"What can this mean?" the old lady cried. "This poor child could never have been a robber!"

"Please do not let the constable drag a sick child off to prison," Miss Rose sobbed.

"My dear," Mrs Maylie replied. "I shall not let them harm a hair of his head. Now, the servant is not even sure if this is the boy he shot. Poor child! He came here for help and he shall have it."

For many weeks after that terrible night, Oliver lay ill with a fever. But slowly he began to feel stronger.

"Thank you for your kindness," he whispered tearfully to Mrs Maylie and Rose. "When I am really better, I shall repay you. I shall work hard for you. I was so ungrateful to the kind gentleman who looked after me before."

"You kept talking about a Mr Brownlow when you

were feverish," Mrs Maylie said, smiling. "When you are better, we shall take you to see him."

Mrs Maylie's promise helped Oliver to improve quickly and the day came at last when he was able to go with her to Mr Brownlow's house. But, to his disappointment, the servants told them that his dear friend had gone abroad.

As the trees began to blossom and the air grew warmer, Oliver went to stay in the countryside with Mrs Maylie and Rose. How peaceful those days were! Every morning, Oliver went to an old gentleman who taught him to read and write. In the afternoon, he walked in the garden with the others. Then, at dusk, Rose played the piano and sang to them. In this happy way, three months passed quickly.

One day, Oliver was out walking alone. As he took a shortcut through the yard of an inn, he bumped into a tall man wrapped in a cloak. This man stared at Oliver in surprise.

"I thought you were dead in a ditch!" the man muttered. "Am I ever going to be rid of you?"

"I… I am sorry, sir," Oliver said, confused by the man's wild look and strange words.

"A curse upon you!" the man said. "If I had had the courage, I could have been free of you in a single night. What are you doing here?"

The man shook his fist and walked towards Oliver. As he raised his arm to hit him, he fell to the ground, trembling and foaming at the mouth. Oliver ran to the inn for help. Then he went back to the cottage as quickly as his legs would carry him.

The next evening, Oliver was busy reading in his little room at the back of the house. As he read, he began to feel sleepy in the late sunshine and he closed his eyes. Suddenly, a voice whispered, "It is him." Oliver woke up in terror and glanced up at the window. There stood Fagin, so close that he could almost have touched him. His eyes peered into the room and met Oliver's.

And beside him, white with anger or fear, stood the tall man he had met outside the inn.

CHAPTER SEVEN
The locket and the ring

Mr Bumble was sitting in the workhouse parlour.

"Are you going to sit there snoring all day?" his wife shouted. "Get up! And get out of my way!"

Mr Bumble walked unhappily up and down the streets. Then he decided to take a drink at one of the inns he had passed. As he went inside, he noticed a tall, dark-haired man, wearing a long cloak.

"I have seen you before, I think?" this man said to Mr Bumble. "You used to work for the parish. You were in charge of its orphans, weren't you?"

"I was," Mr Bumble replied, "until I married the matron of the workhouse. I work there, now."

"I came to this town to find you," the stranger said, "and by chance you have found me! I want some information from you. I shall pay you well. Carry your memory back – let me see – twelve years last winter. It's night and a woman is about to give birth to a boy. The one who went to work for the coffin-maker and ran away to London."

"You mean Oliver Twist!" Mr Bumble cried.

"Indeed," the stranger said. "Now I want to hear about the old nurse who was there when he was born."

"Sally?" Mr Bumble asked. "She died last winter. But I know a woman who was with her when she died."

The man scribbled an address on a piece of paper and gave it to Mr Bumble. "Bring her there tomorrow at nine," he said.

"Who shall I ask for?" Mr Bumble said.

"Monks!" the man replied as he walked away.

The next evening, Mr and Mrs Bumble made their way down to a ruined mill by the river. A small door opened and Monks pulled them inside.

"This is the woman, is it?" Monks asked, bolting the door behind them.

"This is the woman," Mr Bumble replied.

"And she was with the nurse when she died. She knows something about…" the man began.

"…the mother of Oliver Twist," Mrs Bumble finished.

"What did the mother say before she died? That is the first question," Monks said.

"No," Mrs Bumble replied. "The first question is – how much is this information worth? Give me twenty-five pounds and I'll tell you. Not before."

Monks hesitated for a moment. Then he put the coins on the table.

"Sally robbed Oliver's mother. She stole from her corpse," Mrs Bumble said. "It was something that the mother had begged Sally to give to her baby."

"What was it?" Monks asked. "Where is it?"

"Here," Mrs Bumble replied, throwing a leather bag on to the table. "Sally told me about it before she died."

Monks tore open the bag with trembling hands. Inside was a little gold locket containing two locks of hair and a plain gold ring engraved with the name Agnes. He stood up and pushed the table to one side. Then he pulled an iron ring on the floor and opened a large trapdoor. Underneath, they saw a rushing stream. Monks picked up the leather bag, tied a lead weight to it and dropped it into the water.

"If you ever meet me again," he said, "you do not know me. Now get away from here."

CHAPTER EIGHT

A secret conversation

The evening after Monks' meeting with the Bumbles, Nancy went to Fagin's house.

"Bill wants his money for the robbery," she said.

As she spoke, the sound of a man's voice was heard. A few seconds later, Monks appeared in the doorway.

"When did you get back to London?" Fagin asked.

"Two hours ago," Monks replied.

"Did you see him?" Fagin asked.

"I did," Monks said, glancing across at Nancy. "Let me have a word in private."

Fagin took Monks upstairs. While the sound of their footsteps still echoed through the house, Nancy slipped off her shoes, crept upstairs and listened at the door.

"The only proof of the boy's identity lies at the bottom of the river and the old woman who stole it is rotting in her coffin," Monks whispered. "Now I shall have the money that belongs to my young brother, Oliver." He gave a short laugh. "He's staying in a hotel on Hyde Park with a Mrs Maylie! But I don't need you to get him back for me this time. He can never prove who he is now."

Nancy shivered as she heard the last few words. She

tiptoed back downstairs and put on her shoes again.

"How pale you are, Nancy!" Fagin said when he had shown Monks to the front door.

"Let me get back to Sikes," she said sharply. "Give me his money."

With a sigh for every coin he gave her, Fagin counted the money into Nancy's hand. She hurried along the dark streets, breathless and trembling. As soon as Sikes had drunk himself into a deep sleep, she rushed once again from the house. She ran until she reached the small hotel overlooking Hyde Park.

"Be off with you!" the woman at the desk shouted, staring at Nancy's shabby clothes.

"Isn't there anybody here who will carry a message for a poor wretch like me?" Nancy cried. The cook came out when he heard the noise. He took pity on Nancy and a message was taken up to Miss Rose. Soon Nancy found herself in a small room where she waited, trembling from head to foot. At last, Miss Rose came in.

"Tell me why you wish to see me," she said gently.

Her voice was so kind that Nancy burst into tears.

"O lady, lady!" she sobbed, "I am about to put my life, and the lives of others, into your hands. I am the girl that dragged little Oliver back to Fagin's when he was staying with Mr Brownlow. I was forced to do it."

"You!" Rose Maylie exclaimed.

"Yes, me," Nancy replied. "I am that evil girl he has talked of, that lives among thieves. I have stolen for Fagin since I was five years old! The dark alleys and gutters have been my home, and I shall die there."

"I pity you!" Rosie cried.

"They will murder me if they know I am here," Nancy said. "Do you know a man called Monks?"

"No," Rose said. "Who is he?"

"Oliver's older brother," Nancy said. "He is as evil as Fagin. He hoped that Oliver had died in the workhouse. Then he came across him by chance in the street when Mr Brownlow was robbed. He saw the boy's likeness to their father. He's been paying Fagin to keep Oliver because he's too cowardly to have him killed."

"Killed?" Rose asked, horrified. "Why does he wish his brother dead?"

"To steal his inheritance," Nancy said. "Last night, Monks came to see Fagin. He said he had thrown Oliver's only proof of identity to the bottom of a river." Nancy glanced around. "I must go now," she whispered.

"But what can I do with this information?" Rose asked. "And where can I find you if I need you?"

"Every Sunday evening from eleven o'clock until midnight, I will walk on London Bridge – if I am alive," Nancy said. And sobbing, the unhappy girl turned and left the room.

CHAPTER NINE

Nancy pays the price

Rose sat for a long time after Nancy had left.

"I must keep Nancy's secret," she told herself, "but I must do something to help Oliver. He shall have what he is owed. It is only fair!" After a sleepless night, Rose decided to write to Mrs Maylie's son, Harry. As she was trying to decide on the right words, Oliver ran in.

"I have seen Mr Brownlow getting out of a carriage," he gasped. "I was trembling so much that I couldn't even go up to him. What shall I do? What shall I say to him?"

"Perhaps Mr Brownlow is the person to help me now," Rose thought.

In less than five minutes, Rose and Oliver were in a carriage on their way to see him. Rose was shown straight up to the old gentleman's study.

"I have come about a young friend of mine – and yours," she began.

"May I ask his name?" Mr Brownlow said.

"Oliver Twist," Rose replied.

"Miss Maylie," he said, "if you can tell me anything that will change my opinion of that boy, tell me now."

"He is a child of a noble nature and a warm heart," Rose said, blushing. "I have come to tell you all the terrible things that have happened to him since he was kidnapped not far from your house."

Mr Brownlow listened in horror. "The poor child!" he said when she had finished. "Where is he now?"

"He is waiting in the carriage," Rose said.

Without another word, Mr Brownlow rushed outside. He brought Oliver up to his room, shouting for his housekeeper who hugged Oliver and sobbed loudly.

"What shall we do now?" Rose whispered to Mr Brownlow.

"We must not be hasty," he whispered back. "Unfortunately, we have no proof against Monks. He is not a thief like the rest of them. We shall ask Nancy where we can find him." He paused and looked at Rose. "It is five days until we meet Nancy on London Bridge," he said. "Oliver must not know about this – not yet."

As the days passed slowly by, Nancy grew thin and pale with worry. When the church clock struck eleven that first Sunday evening, Sikes and Fagin were deep in conversation as Nancy got ready to go out.

"Nance!" Sikes cried, "Where yer going?"

"I'm not well," she replied. "I need some air."

"Then put yer head out of the winder," Sikes said.

Nancy walked towards the door. Sikes got up and locked it. Then he pulled off Nancy's bonnet and pushed her into a chair. Nancy struggled and begged until the clock struck twelve. At last, he left her alone.

"She is tired of him," Fagin thought as he hurried home. "I wonder if she has found new friends? I shall ask one of the boys to follow her."

The following Sunday, the clock of St Paul's was chiming a quarter to midnight as two figures walked across London Bridge. One of them was Nancy and the other a boy who slunk along in the deepest shadows. Two minutes after midnight, Miss Rose and Mr Brownlow arrived in a carriage. They got out and walked towards Nancy. "Not here!" she whispered. "I am afraid. We'll go down to the river."

"Now listen to me," Mr Brownlow said as they reached the water's edge. "We must ask Monks to tell us the truth. How will we know him?"

"He is tall," Nancy whispered, "and always looks over his shoulder as he walks. His eyes are sunk deep in his head. His face is dark, like his hair and eyes. He is about twenty-six years old. His lips and hands are often discoloured with bites from his teeth because he has fits. He always wears a large cloak. On his neck is a large…"

"…red mark like a burn or a scald!" Mr Brownlow said quietly. "I think I may know him. I am not sure. It is not the same name."

He stood silent for a moment. Then he looked kindly at Nancy.

"What can I do for you in return?" he asked.

"Nothing, sir," she said sadly. "I am past all help. I hate my life but I cannot leave it now. Good night!"

The boy in the shadows waited until Nancy had gone. Then he ran back to Fagin's house as fast as his legs would carry him.

A few days later, when everybody else was asleep, Fagin sat in the light of a flickering candle. His face was so pale and his eyes so red that he looked more like a ghost than a man. He bit the long black nails of his right hand with the few teeth he had left. The bell interrupted his thoughts. "At last!" Fagin muttered.

Sikes came into the room and threw a bundle on to the table. Fagin locked it in a cupboard and sat down, staring hard at his friend.

"Say wot you've got to say!" Sikes cried at last.

Fagin shook one of the boys awake. "Tell him about Nancy," he ordered.

The sleepy boy repeated all that he had seen and heard on London Bridge. Sikes jumped angrily to his feet and rushed out.

"You won't be… be too violent with her, will you, Bill?" Fagin called after him.

Sikes did not answer. He ran all the way home and locked the door behind him. Then he woke Nancy up. He grasped her by the head and throat with one hand and dragged her from the bed.

"Do not kill me, Bill!" Nancy begged. "I have done nothing to hurt you."

Sikes picked up his pistol and hit Nancy twice. She staggered and fell, blinded by the blood running from a deep cut on her forehead. Nancy pulled herself to her knees and began to pray. But as she did so, Sikes picked up a wooden club and beat her to death.

CHAPTER TEN
The truth at last

Some days later, while the police were still looking for Sikes, Mr Brownlow sat in his study with Monks.

"You are my father's oldest friend," Monks shouted. "How dare you kidnap me in the street! What do you want from me?"

"I recognised you from Nancy's description!" Mr Brownlow said. "You have not changed very much since you were a child. You have a brother called Oliver. When I whispered his name to you just now in the street, it was enough to make you to come here with me."

"No!" Monks cried. "I have no brother!"

"Let me remind you of the past," Mr Brownlow said sadly. "Your father, as you have just said, was my dearest friend. He was forced to marry your mother and they were very unhappy. After they separated, your father met a widower, a Mr Fleming, who had two daughters. He fell in love with one of them – Agnes – and promised to marry her when he was free."

"What has this to do with me?" Monks asked.

"When your father died suddenly, he left no will. All his money went to you and your mother," Mr Brownlow said. "But just before he died, he came to see me."

"I did not know that," Monks said with sudden interest.

"He brought me the portrait he had painted of Agnes," Mr Brownlow said.

"Is that all?" Monks sneered.

"I met Oliver by chance," Mr Brownlow said. "He looked so much like Agnes Fleming that I was determined to find out more about him. When he disappeared, I tried to find you, hoping you could tell me where he was. I even followed you abroad. I did not know you had stolen him from me!"

"You cannot prove anything," Monks cried.

"I know every word that you have spoken to Fagin," Mr Brownlow said. "Shadows on the wall have heard your whispers and brought them to me. Poor Nancy. Now she is dead and you are partly to blame."

"No, no!" Monks cried. "That had nothing to do with me."

"Will you tell the truth, then?" the old gentleman asked, "and give Oliver his inheritance? It will not be long before Sikes is arrested. He will give Fagin away. Everybody will hear how you paid Fagin to keep the boy."

Monks paced up and down, his face angry and evil.

"I promise," he said at last.

A few days later, Mrs Maylie and Rose took Oliver to

see Mr Brownlow. The poor boy jumped with fright when he saw the tall man wrapped in a cloak sitting in the corner of the room.

"That is the man I bumped into at the inn!" he cried, "and the man who peered into my room with Fagin."

"This is your half-brother, Mr Edward Leeford," Mr Brownlow said gently, "known as Monks."

He put his arm around Oliver and stared at Monks.

"Now tell us the truth as you promised!" he said.

Monks scowled at the trembling boy.

"Before my father died, he wrote a will," he said. "In it, he left most of his money to Agnes and her child – you," he said, looking at Oliver angrily. "My mother burnt the will."

Mr Brownlow turned towards Rose. "Do you know this young lady, sir?" he asked Monks.

"I have never seen you before," Rose said, trembling.

"I have often seen you," Monks replied. "Agnes had a sister who was very young when Oliver was born. You are that sister. My mother hated you as much as she hated Agnes. She told everybody you had been born outside marriage. After your father died, she made sure you lived a miserable life with a poor family."

"Until Mrs Maylie saw me and adopted me," Rose whispered, tears in her eyes.

"Don't weep, my child," said Mrs Maylie. "Look, here,

who waits and longs to clasp you in his arms, poor child!"

"I shall never call you aunt!" Oliver said, as he threw his arms around Rose's neck. "You shall be my own, dear sister." And he cried at last with happiness.

The stories of these people are nearly over and what little is left can be told in a few simple words. Rose married Mrs Maylie's son, Harry, three months later, about the same time that Mr Brownlow adopted Oliver. The dear boy took only half of his inheritance, and insisted on giving the other half to Monks. Sikes was chased by the police to an old warehouse and hung to death on his own rope as he tried to swing across the rooftops. And Fagin? He was hanged, too – watched by a large crowd outside the prison.